POETRY
of
CHRISTMAS

How Holy and Jolly the Night Jesus Christ was Born

CHARLES MWEWA

DEDICATION

For my family and friends, wherever they may be, Merry Christmas!

CONTENTS

AUTHOR'S WORD

Poetry of Christmas

In this book, *Poetry of Christmas: How Holy and Jolly the Night Jesus Christ was Born*, I draw from my other publications, such as *Poetry the Best of Charles Mwewa, Valley of Roses, Fairer than Grace,* and others, and bring together all my favorite Christmas poems. Some poems in this book arc sccing their first publication. All in all, the book brings balance between the excessive celebration of Christmas *without* Christ Himself in it, and the return to the Lord of Christmas, who is Christ Jesus.

It is important to endear all the lyrics and themes of this period, which has been recognized all over the world as the "Most Wonderful Season" of the year. We should, therefore, be dutybound to mention Santa (also known as Santa Claus, Father Christmas, Saint

Nicholas, Saint Nick, or Kris Kringle), reindeers, candy canes, ugly sweaters, snow, snowman, mistletoe, Christmas trees, jingle bells, Christmas lights, etc. But we should also remember that all these thematic characters exist because of "Christ" in *Christ*mas. Otherwise, we are left with only a "mas" of debauchery, carousing and overspending.

Having clarified that, Christmas must be a time to ponder, wonder, and be astounded by the works of love and reflections of peace. As the angels declared, Christmas brought peace to the world. At Christmas, let us dance, feast and also reflect on God's goodness towards mankind.

Merry Christmas!

POETRY OF CHRISTMAS

Promised Child

Unto us a child is given
The error of the world will be forgiven
Kings and rulers at His feet will bow
His majesty, though not of this world will be
wow
He will live faultlessly, doing miracles wherever
he goes
And bring glory to God in whatever He does
For unto us a Baby child is born
An' unto us He will sit on His holy throne
Nations will before Him pay homage
And He will dominate all as He comes of age
Glory, glory to God for His reign is eternal;
Thanks be to God He will save all internal.

Grace to Mary

The loves of the heavens to this girl visit
Oh, how blessed to be the one for this chosen
The majesty of the highest to this lad do solicit
When first introduced to her, her sense did bid
frozen
Till she realized that it was all of grace
And to God she gave praise in that place.
Oh, Mary, you are honored among all women
And from the mouths of all men
You will forever be the Mother of God
The womb that brought to earth divine gold.
Praise be to the heaven above the heavens
For your benedictions come to us in sevens.

Emmanuel is Noel

Noel, noel, noel, noel, new things He's
brought
Oh, Emmanuel, goods with you you've got
For humanity has received a double of your
worth
And blessings you've given, all blessings to
earth
Halleluiah, God in the flesh He has become
For angels in the highest do sing a glory hum
The celebrations of the host who Him worship
To showcase the best of heaven's
entrepreneurship
Oh, man, what a wonder, a benediction of
hope
How wonderful this symphony, this divine
scope
For from hence, all creatures shall ascribe Him
Lord
For in His mouth, proceeds a sharpness that's
of a sword.

Brown Christmas Tree

Oh, look, this Christmas tree is very brown
It's with royal sheds in shapes of a crown
My daughter said this year, we need a tree
Adorned with silvery ribbons tied in three
It tells us of the Holy Trinity
And their love given to infinity
For to us a Son was perfectly born
Announced by jovial angels with a horn
Oh, how joyous this moment to party
The sound music around it is hearty
We will hear the nativity story
Proudly proclaimed, "To God be the glory."

No Gifts this Christmas

I want no early gift this Christmas
I will attend no concert nor mass
I want only a very simple gift
I don't mind if it is only a thrift
I will think about the wonder of the earth
And the brilliance of the highest heaven
For this year's Christmas is so special
I give myself to Him as a holy vessel.

Mistletoe Blues

Listening to the song about the mistletoe
I wanted to bring some romance to the show
I placed it under a bushel of a burning lantern
Then I sat silently and expecting for my turn
Even in this atmosphere of brimming cheer
I was still within gripped by a ravaging fear
Then changed were my mistletoe blues
The Sun of Righteousness is Good News.

Christmas in the Kalahari

I wondered how they would celebrate Noel
How they would announce it without a bell
Would Kalahari' heat dump their mood
Would it destroy all the fruits and fresh food
Then came music oozing out of the sands
And flashes of glories carried in their hands
"Christmas is here," the trumpet gave a sound
And from nowhere, dancers gathered around.
The I saw Santa's camel called Chansar
Whom the North's reindeer is Prancer
Ran ahead of the rogous Igbonsar
Who carries the Artic demeanor of Dancer
The benevolent, shying 'tcholixen
Was next with stashes of gifts akining Vixen
And they came beneath Father Christmas' Isha
Whose samesake is christened Dosher
The aerial raving of the snowy lands, Cupid
Has a likadesical kinsake in Notshepid
And edging the snow-mover, Dona.
They urged it on to be like the florious Donner
But it was the flawless, moodless, Ifondomedt,
The tantalizingly effluent one, a type of Comet
Who held on to the fondly praised Czarivzen,

And as agile as the North Pole's Blitzen,
They escorted Santa's train led by Zebroff,
The archally of the red-nosed Rudolph.

To Jerusalem for Christmas

This Christmas, I want to go to Jerusalem
I want to experience the Peace of Salem
To frolic in bliss in the midst of the war
And change the mood to glow from gore
For the Prince who brings peace is born
Let us lift up with gladness our blessed horn
Let us celebrate the end of all grievous souls
For our destiny now Christ Jesus controls
And from hence, the government is His
With Him, all ephemeral foes we'll whiz.

Lights at Christmas

The light burns brightly to the end.
All things look good and very calm.
And wild flowers invade the land
In the presence of mistletoe.

It is Christmas Day in Sameland
Children will open their presents
And sit rounding the twinkling tree
In red oversized pajamas.

This season is very special
And the songs are very unique
People everywhere share in joy
To bring true peace in a vexed world.

These parcels of assorted gifts
Long gathered carefully in thrift
And in malls the jingle bells ring
While kids hum from carols singing.

The poor and needy will reckon
With lack and shortage that beckon
But with help from joyful Santa
They will receive gifts and Fanta.

Music in the Sky

I am amazed how that
Above the clouds
That are above a gigantic ocean
Beats resounding melodies
In symphony of superb tunes
And sweet voice of Celine Deon,
And the electric vocals of Richie,
And the vibrancy of Cocker
Together with the beaming
Eloquence of Dolly-
How that *these* music go
On playing in the landless paths
In those heavens far above.
The sound so beautiful
In those snowy azures,
Bringing earthly pleasure.
These ecstasies are heavily pried for
When the listening becomes intense
And these beats flap the hips of the engine.
There is music in heaven
Bright and beautiful
Drawing a soothing feeling of laughter.

In these skies the busy-ness of life
And the pressure of brewing
Are all swallowed up
Compacted and recycled
And hearts beat in chorus.
Nearing the soils
Melodies begin to faint,
These sweet waves,
Softer than the soul -
And still, there is music in the sky.

Sweet Name

Sweet is your name to my memory
Smooth to my clean-shaven cheeks.
Did I tell you I knew about you
When in sense and word we rhymed?
You were my morning brightening star
A song I sang when I knew not how.
I saw your face always in phases,
When you smiled without blinking,
And spoke without moving upper lips.

Sound are my dreams when I fall asleep
Saying your name repeatedly and softly.
You were right when you kissed me
And not wrong when I held you back.
But it is your heart that I adore;
Your smiles that dropped spotless love –
For while many friends I have had,
To find one like you is truly hard.

Broken Lullaby

Stranger your tongue and tone is a broken
lullaby
For before we had time to talk, we said
goodbye.
I have met many who look like you, and have
said "hi!"
Only to discover they are not you when they
sigh.
I have tried to forget about you and reach very
high
But when your frame illuminates mine, I say,
"my, my!"
We were like sister and a brother when we
shared a pie
But you knew to me you were not just but
another guy.
One thing you didn't want me to do, I don't
know why
You never let me stroke your knuckles or let
me try.
You were an angel who brightened my very
blue sky
And carved the wings with which I was able to
fly.

Words Fail Me

On this Christmas, it's you I remember,
I pay my due credit in the middle of December
Oh, Lord God, you created me with all tools
Yet words fail me to declare all your rules
For thou art our God, the only true God
For thou art unique, O Transcendent Lord
For thou art the owner, master, True Sir
And all creation worships you, near and far
Thou art our Holy Father in all wise
For you carest, provideth, and chastise
Oh, Supreme Lord, Despotes, O Kurios
Our All in all, the Almighty, O Theos.

Indescribable YOU

To us, You're the Sun,
To God, His Baby Son,
How can I praise You,
O Sweetest of Heaven,
You,
who dwells in unapproachable haven,
You, who is terrific,
prolific,
and truly omnific
Thy creation, magnific,
and altogether beautific!

Ultimate Christmas Prayer

Let my future be uncertain, undefined, unclear,
So, I can know the power of Your convincing
faith;
Let the sharpest pain lunge through my
bleeding flesh,
So, I can appreciate the pleasure of Your
healing hand;
Let me suffer loss, be destitute and reel from
misery,
So, I can understand the meaning of divine
providence;
Let my plans be frustrated, my dreams fail to
come true,
So, I can stay true to what You have purposed
for my life;
Let me experience disappointment, utter
humiliation,
So, I should never put my trust in my own
shrewdness;
Let me be rejected, dejected and totally
offended,
So, I should learn to love those who despise
me;

Let me fail lamentably, suffer invectives and
insults,
So, I should endear every victory that comes
from You;
Let me taste lack, being broke beyond
penniless despair,
So, I should know that every good gift comes
from above;
Let me go naked, be vulnerable, homeless and
needy,
So, I can crave to abide under the shadow of
Your wings;
Let somebody else win, best me, come out
ahead of me,
So, I should be contented with the success that
is Yours;
Let me die a bitter, painful and an agonizing
death,
So, I may wake up whole, in blissful, joyous by
and by.

Holy Grace

You have delivered me from their wolverine
claws
You have spoken to their minds and hearts
And You have silenced the trouble-makers
Surely, their grasp is broken, their will
shattered
They all, will not for me trouble make
Lord, I am assured of Your never-ending love
I am satisfied with Your everlasting kindness
You have shown me mercy and preserved me
Also, I have watched in the morning hours
And have heart Your tender voice saying,
"It is over, it is over my son, you're free!"
O bless the Lord, bless the Lord O my soul
And do not forget His benefits and good
works
For as sure as day and night will reveal
themselves
So has the Good Lord manifested His good
grace.
Oh, the sounds of this holy day, this hope to
endear
Oh, the whispers of noel, Christ's love to us is
dear.

Essence of Presence

We have wondered away from Your presence
We thought of floundering Your holy essence
Yet, not for a moment did You forsake us
Not for a moment You withdrew Jesus
Father, You saw us when we did not pray
You were acquainted with our vainly play
You did not forget us, not even once
You did not grant our enemy a chance
On our knees, will we bow before this Cross
Not for a time, will we stray from its course.

Ode to Moments before Christmas

My soul wonders like one lost in deep jungle
I seek for peace my heart so longs for
When I awake, my worries are before me
When I say I should hide, behold I am still
here

Taken by the wiles of the world
Pricked by the thorns of the world
Tricked by the lies of the world
Stricken by the tries of the world

My only recourse is to you, dear Lord
When I picked up that Holy Script,
Oh, even in this I am deeply enchanted,
How that the Child so simple, breeds solutions
divine

How that man in his desperation forsakes him
That woman has begged for fullness apart
from him
That in our humiliation we have not gone to
him
And our own frailty of life has not discovered
him

For me, I toss in bed for hours, hours without
end
I reason in the secrets of my thoughts without
end
I reflect on the myth of the coming end
Oh, who will decipher beginning from end

For there is no peace one finds in earthly glory
No-one has returned to tell of the end of life
Indeed, we may desire to live but for this life
Yet, within my soul there is faith divine

Within the concourses of my doubts, I find
belief
Within the worries of life, I find a way open
Within this hole, this emptiness of my heart
Within this search my heart hears a voice

A Child is born
A King is given
He will reign supreme
His rules shall never end

I once walked the dry steps of the print of
God
Heard the waterfall of glorified saints sing and
pray
And led a throng of worshippers to the throne
of mercy;
Oh, how my being rejoices for a chance of
this.

My soul said, indulge for tomorrow is illusive
Drink and be merry and shun the fear of death
Drown yourself in the pleasure of life
And forget about the fear of the good Lord.

My own views were clear and I said I will
attempt all
I will find out what is it that the wicked have
mastered,
I will go where they learn and observe them
I will pretend I have no knowledge of the Holy
One

I struggled to find my hand at their best skill
and power
For with simplicity, they acquired pleasure
And with sophistication they braved hearts and
souls
And with plain gain they indulged to the very
essence.

At no time did they mention of the wrath of
Judgment
No-one dared to define the end of all sinners
For to them, the end comes with the last
breath,
And they hope only for what mind and brain
demand.

They sang of songs of pure earthly joys
They planned for their sons and daughters
They acquired great wealth with all their might
They knew they would die someday.

In my desperation I also almost joined them
I almost envied their wanton carousing,
I said in my heart, "Just a bit, a small taste,"
Till in the center of my soul I heard a voice

A Child is born
A King is given
He will reign supreme
His rules shall never end

I saw that they had a thought of the future,
their future
They abhorred any who dared mentioned God
And they looked down upon those who
believed
For to them, only shallow minds contemplate
God.

Many times, I saw sense in their machinations
Their plans prospered and they lived in luxury
Their ingenuity brought forth innovations
Their brilliance revolutionized technologies.

I said to myself, this is how life should be
approached
Without the bondage of a faith that never
rewards
The worries of the omissions to an invisible
God
And the fears of the Judgment to come.

Just when I began to be comfortable, my soul
failed me
My achievements became trophies of a
desperate winner
And all those defences I knew kept me safe
Only gave me more sleepless nights and great
perturbation

I have come to a place of reconciliation, a
place of penance
When I think that I have a legacy, alas, it has
no foundation
When I say I will depend of the books I have
written
In that I find a small joy and a begging
ferment.

For man, there is nothing good but to eat and
drink
To enjoy the flowers growing naturally in
nature
And to work with one`s hands to perfection
While God lends us all a brief existence on
earth.

And on that brief existence I had thoughts, too
It has a sorrow so deep, a sadness unhealable
It shudders reason, and frustrates the essence
of joy
Till I walked past a church, and I heard a
singing voice:

A Child is born
A King is given
He will reign supreme
His rules shall never end

I walked by the elegant cemetery where death
is pensive
There I saw the frailty of man`s machinations
I heard the unsaid silences of the traps of
living without God
And my heart became a circus of troubled
waters.

Who has wisdom to read the invisible ink
To understand that it is a chance of naught
To peg our hopes in things we do
To forget the mercies of the Holy One

Deep down my heart I knew the answer, only
imperfect
I knew that from the cheapness of God`s love
Flows the priceless trophy of life`s desires
For which man may be saved and delivered

It is travesty, that weak men have abused the
grace of God
That money and materialism have ended real
prayer
And all live only to please their bellies
Without giving God His glory

I now understand what I should do: not
tomorrow
I will tell God of all my weaknesses: he heals
souls
I will disclose my deepest ambitions: he will
bear with me
And I will ask for his forgiveness: he is slow to
anger

Oh, God, add more hours to my whimpering
years
Do not give my soul to the shackles of the
burning hell,
And let me tell of your wonders like you are
Even when I need it only for a short time

In the shadows of my intentions, I recalled
That God is good, he abounds in mercy and
compassion
He will forsake not those who constantly think
on him
And a rising anthem wrung through my
meditating voice:

A Child is born
A King is given
He will reign supreme
His rules shall never end

And in these my daily toils, teach me to see the
end
For in much toiling, I am still very empty
And in much anticipation, I gain only
frustration
As in one duty there is more tasks waiting

Give me a simple life to enjoy, a simple life to
guard
Give me love for those things that matter to
you
And the knowledge of those things that have
value
Since only through you can there be true peace

I have three or four adventures I would like to
fulfill
Oh Lord, you know they are in line but only of
grace
They are the childish ambitions of my life
And if I should achieve them, I know they are
vanity

Yet give them to me, nevertheless
What is this white which my body so desire
What is this power that my mind will cheer
And this law that I may be nobly sure

In this white, I will know you have been fair to
mankind
In this power I will bring to you the glories of
earth
And in these I will build for all nations a godly
rest;
For in these vanities, let your true wisdom
reign

When I pray, I seek for highs higher than
spirits
When I pray, I see with a clearer lens
When I pray, I heal from all anxieties
When I pray, even wrath turns to God`s glory

So quickly, Lord, you've turned my mourning
into dancing
So fast, ferocious tides have turned into
calming breezes
So good I feel the embers of joy pummeling in
my pulses
So clear, within me came a sweet, soothing
voice:

A Child is born
A King is given
He will reign supreme
His rules shall never end

Jesus Christ

In coming He chose us, promises fulfilled
In living He loved us, all sickness He healed
In dying He saved us, all sin paid for in full
In rising He freed us, for He's faithful
In ascending He held us, many rooms to create
In sitting He prays us, the way is straight
In returning He gathers us, in Him we grow
In judging He rewards us, in Him we glow
In separating He blest us, hearts at ease
In reigning He changes us, His rule is in peace.

Works of Charity

For the sake of your secret blessings, don`t pay
There is a rewarder of those who dare to pray
Whose right hand does not interfere with left
And when they gave, they quickly left.

Blessed are those who must not show off
When all they did was help the sufferings of
Those who had nothing even to repay
For all the gifts received when they pray.

It is better to give your gifts in secret
Where no-one can dig through the concrete
And hope to find out that it was you
Who gave the way of the blessed few.

God honors the gifts given in love
The ones which are not announced above
So that no-one can know the givers
And such receive all of God`s favors.

Cheerful Giver

God loves a cheerful giver;
The one who gives for a purpose,
The purpose greater than just showing off.
There are people in this world who need help.
There are people in need of our help every day
And these people should be the genuine
recipients of our gifts.
We should be careful that we are not heaping
rewards on those who already have plenty
Or on those who are bent on building their
own empires in the name of God.
God has made it very clear that our giving
Should be in secret and not in public making a
publicity stunt of it.
When we do such, we pre-empt God`s ability
to bless us,
And in that way too, we receive the praises of
men
And miss out on true divine rewards.
Seek, and again I say, seek to give,
Especially to those in desperate need,
And God will surely bless you.

Mercy and Grace

Mercy withheld from us what we deserve
Grace gave to us what we did not deserve
Lord, it was mercy that saved us from hell
And grace did send us to heaven's well
By mercy I knew that sin's shame was gone
And by grace, I knew that God's will was done
Mercy, how wonderful You sealed the hole
Grace, how amazing Your rule made me whole
So, I bow, with truth that mercy found me
I worship, grace gave me eyes now I see.

Wisdom of Christ

O, the infinite wisdom of Christ Jesus,
The Leader
His supreme prudence in world harvest
His beauty, unmatched – Lily of the Valley,
Rose of Sharon
His tremendous creativity in creation, yet Man
of Sorrows
O, Merciful High Priest, Messiah who is Prince
A Nazarene, yet King of all kings
He has overcome, O Lord God Omnipotent
And His name is above all names.

A Christian Life

My God, do live a Christian life for me
For in myself, I try and fail daily
My flesh works but to please itself only
So, the things I want to do I don't do
Dead desires in my body form a queue
My faculties compete for the gaudy
If I should say that I don't sin, I lie
And the truth of God is far from being nigh
Only in Christ can I live in purity
Dear Spirit, be my steadfast surety.

Holier, Lowlier

Oh, that I may be but emptier, lowlier,
And be to my God a vessel holier,
Oh, that I may be to all sin, slower
And to kneel down before His throne, lower,
Oh, that I may to righteousness be, a slave
And to dying to sinful flesh, fast and brave
Oh, that I may pray, daily, and longer
And to grow in my faith a lot stronger
Oh, that I may be unnoticed, unknown,
And be filled but with Christ, and Christ alone.

Christmas Fun-Fair

I went with my family to a Christmas Fun-Fair
at Woodbine
It was the first time Cutera and I rode into
many a show-fine
Then I remembered how, Father, it must
please You to see,
How that us earthly parents can for our
children there be,
But You are more than a parent, You are a
caring Father,
May my days be spent caring for those for me
You gather.
May the joys of Christmas never end,
Like Baby Jesus, on You we depend.

Fairer than the Moon

Oh, how beautiful Thou art, O Lord, my God,
how beautiful
Thy countenance shines brightly, Thy grace is
bountiful
And fairer than the moon or the sun in their
azure glory
Even more attractive than the angels in all
their flurry
Thou art God – Father, Spirit and Son – all an
intricate Triune
More than medals and trophies, I own Thee
only, as mine.

Darling of Heaven

You are most awesome, O Darling of Heaven
How bountiful are the blessings You have
given
The seasons, each blossom in its orbit
faithfully
The oceans retain their boundaries lawfully
And the elements are neither too hot nor too
cold
For sure in heaven above, there is a caring
God.

Heavens Declare

The heavens declare the glory of God
The moon speaks of His mercy and truth
And the stars announce his eternal grace.
The clouds acknowledge His kindness
And the sun supplies His everlasting light.

Valley of Roses

My best Father, my dearest Creator,
For You are magnificently gorgeous,
And majestically glorious in splendor.
You're the universe's endearing Darling,
A City where beautiful is harvested,
In Your favor, my dues have been met,
Your presence, is the zest sustaining me.
You, Lord, You're my Valley of Roses,
For I bow to none other or any bosses.

City Called Beautiful

O, my God, today is a day of fast, a day of
humility
To You and only You I come, in the name of
Jesus,
I have never trusted in any other, thing or
person
My eyes have only been for You, Lord my
deliverer.
For who can save either by His words or His
might?
Only You, my Lord, my Savior, You save
brilliantly,
You prepare a sumptuous table for my
enjoyment,
You set Your favors, in the City Called
Beautiful.
For in my heart is born Your Son, blessed and
holy
And to this world, He will bring cheer and
jolly.

Almost Winter

It's almost winter,
and the snow already fell.
she rushes home in a sprinter,
to escape the gaping shell
of an outpour across the Arctic;
I received a call from Antarctic,
bidding me to let go
of the already feigning foe;
oh, fear, she'snt gripped by it;
nay, nor the love of couples
can be sacrificed on merit,
but we'll be nimble and supple
for the sake of winter,
he may tolerate a splinter.
Surely, the memories of bliss
will filter this Christmas
and as friends gather in the snow
We shall jingle more bells for now.

Christmas Tree for Cuteravive

For Christmas, she wants a Christmas tree
She asked for it in rings of three
First time, she didn't know it was not for free
But when it was explained, she did agree

This Christmas, we'll buy a tree in November
So, it will be ready for Christmas in December
We'll keep it indoors till end of September;
We'll let it become dry, then turn it into ember

Oh, how happy she was when it lit with lights
How enjoyable her life beamed with delight
We will always get a tree for Cuteravive
And provide love for the season to thrive.

Many Faces of Santa

The many faces and states of Santa,
To the thirsty, he tastes like Fanta;
His Northern name is Santa Claus,
To children, he's a saint with no flaw;
In Europe, Africa, he's Father Christmas,
And he connects nations like an isthmus;
Devotees call him simply as Saint Nicholas,
He cradles the homeless with brain ticklers;
But his street name is Saint Nick,
Everywhere he goes, he does the same trick;
And, of course, you know him as Kris Kringle,
For he reveals his giftsack with jingles.

Snowman Dancing

On December 21, I made a snowman
The next day, he moved, with no man
But I thought that I was dreaming
To be sure, I trimmed his nose, breaming
On December 23, I found his arm broken,
But no-one said they got him shaken.
Early on Christmas morning
His face was reddish, adorning;
A child said, "Snowman was dancing,"
When I looked, surely, he was glancing.

Flawless Anthem

Come and let us celebrate
the birth of God the Son,
Jesus Christ, the beautiful,
who for our inglorious past
became our glorious future,
who for our quest to honor
became humanity's dishonor,
and who gave His hallowed name
for a curse to bring us
before the holy and elevated God,
our Father,
and the Holy Spirit, our Guarantor.
For Christmas is He
and He is Christmas,
to the majesty of His being,
the being of His grandeur,
from generations to generations,
let Him be adored, forever,
in this our merriest of Christmases,
may His flawless anthem ring.

Holy and Jolly the Night

Rarely does that which is holy
Also becomes a beauty, jolly
Rarely does the holy divine
Also takes on the finite,
And from it to recline.
Rarely does He who is magnificent
And altogether excellent
Would for fallen humanity descent
As a Baby in a manger
And them to save from danger
Oh, *holly*, how *holly*
Oh, jolly, how jolly
The night Jesus Christ was born
In that day he forfeited his throne.

Poetry of Christmas

The Christmas atmosphere is sensational
People's laughter and smiles, so intentional
The lights lit brightly in the snowy streets
Candy canes are offered generously as treats
Choirs dressed in cheers sing lovely carols
Gifts are shopped day and night in barrels
Thre is a cheery and sentimental tingle
As seasonal bells rave in a rhythmic jingle
The greenish gold in rumblings of red
In cards and tumblers lively spread
And this mood can only be described as jolly
The melody from churches' sanctums is holy
Even that devilish conman, that Grinch
Is making donations without sparing an inch
Hope will be built in human hearts tonight
From memorable admirations to delight
Ave Maria chorus romp the Catholic mass
Kids simply love this Baby Christ Christmas
No Protestant is upset by the statue of Mary
Even a long-held adversary is treated as a fairy
No-one seems to be in a hurry, all do tarry
Gentle eyes flashily gaze at a night starry
As siblings wiggle in ugly cozy sweaters
Listening merrily to the tune, "Hate Eaters."
This Christmas is like music on replay
How I wish that it must be like this everyday.

Simple Christmas, Darling

I know what you're thinking, Darling
And of late, we have been quarreling
Because you want a lavish Christmas
And I know that it is not my business
To impose upon you a simple gesture
But you despised my efforts as a vesture
And you switched off the Christmas tree
Because it was cheap and almost free
You said that our house had no chimney
That it lacked the aura and magic of Disney
And you didn't talk to me for weeks
Indeed, your silence very loudly it speaks
But I know that since last Christmas Day
When we watched that Christmas play
We have been the happiest this year
Although we lived a simple life here,
In a smaller apartment, sleeping simple
Easting, cleaning and sweeping civil,
We've spent less, and consumed healthy
And let's admit, have been a bit wealthy.
Yes, Santa did not have to find socks
But we always left outside an empty box
You still drove in your Mercedes Benz
But I priced all my cheerful friends
I know you plan to buy costly pajamas

And at the same time go to Bahamas,
But I think that the heart is what matters
To give love is better than multiple flatters
And to sleep on the floor with peace
Is comfier than a feast with caprice.
That's why this Christmas, I beg you,
Let us change altogether the menu;
Let's have more love and less things,
Let's enjoy simple pleasured blessings,
Especially, as our last-born said today,
"If I have money, to the poor I'll it away,"
And I think she has a very good point,
I think that helping the poor could count,
Even as many are hurting without shelter
A gift to the poor can figure out better.
For me, I can enjoy even a cheap pen
Overspending on gadgets or even VPN
Should not define this festive season
I know that this is not pressing a reason,
But Jesus did receive gold and incense
And some myrrh in receiving sets,
We also know that people matter to Him
Just as precious metals did to any Jewish;
So, if we bring our hearts filled with joy
And a few necessary gifts like a kid's toy,
We can still call it the Happy Holiday
And enjoy sweet honey like an apiology.
My dear, what matters to a gift is intent,

To give love and hope is a true present,
And it shouldn't be bought at the Tiffany;
I can be anywhere one is putting money.
A present from a dollar store with love,
And a wish made for loved ones with luck
Are better than a sacrifice of many bucks,
Only to emerge after New Year penniless.
Therefore, I want to wish you the merriest
And looking to the future, the aeriest,
Have the cheapest and yet the loveliest,
A meaningful Christmas, and funniest!

ABOUT THE AUTHOR

Award-Winning, Best-Selling Author, Charles Mwewa (LLB; BA Law; BA Ed; LLM), is a prolific researcher, poet, novelist, lawyer, law professor and Christian apologist and intercessor. Mwewa has written no less than 100 books and counting in every genre and has exhibited his works at prestigious expos like the Ottawa International Book Expo and is the winner of the Coppa Awards for his signature publication, *Zambia: Struggles of My People*.
Mwewa and his family live in the Canadian Capital City of Ottawa.

SELECTED BOOKS BY THIS AUTHOR

INDEX

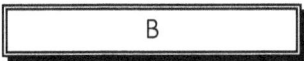